T0208922

JESUS' RAPTURE PROPHECY THE LAST DAY

Daniel Farey

WESTBOW
PRESS®
A DIVISION OF THOMAS NELSON
& ZONDERVAN

WestBow Press books may be ordered through booksellers or by contacting:

WestBow Press
A Division of Thomas Nelson & Zondervan
1663 Liberty Drive
Bloomington, IN 47403
www.westbowpress.com
1 (866) 928-1240

Scripture taken from the King James Version of the Bible.

ISBN: 978-1-9736-9560-8 (sc)
ISBN: 978-1-9736-9561-5 (hc)
ISBN: 978-1-9736-9559-2 (e)

Library of Congress Control Number: 2020911940

Print information available on the last page.

WestBow Press rev. date: 06/30/2020

CONTENTS

INTRODUCTION

Many in organized religion and theology have written about the Rapture over the past two millennium since Jesus ascended to the right hand of God but none have discerned the correct explication from the Bible. This book will focus on the resurrection of humanity, commonly referred to as the Rapture, the second greatest event to come in history next to the resurrection of Jesus Christ. Jesus set the example as the first begotten of the dead and every soul since Creation, good and bad, will be resurrected.

This book is structured as a reference manual and will use the King James Holy Bible as the predominate resource for authenticity and referent. Have your KJV Bible handy as the scripture I refer to in this explication will be from it. The KJV Bible is the most correct transliteration from the Hebrew and Greek to English.

The predominate explications of the Rapture are some form of pre, mid or post of the seven-year Tribulation resurrection which are all supposition, conjecture and symbolism that are focused mainly from the Apostle Paul's prophecies and the lie that the church will not go through the Tribulation which it will. For some unexplained reason they have ignored the simple explanation from Jesus.

What I will teach you is that which the Holy Ghost has taught me and is so simple and straightforward that it shreds all the pride filled

Tribulation Rapture fictitious explications. I belong to no church or religion and have attended no college of theology. Diligent study alone with prayer produced this book as well as my previous book. Read Matthew 6:6.

In my book, Testimonials of a Biblical Christian a Nonreligious Perspective of the Holy Bible, I have a chapter titled The Third Woe Revelation Hereafter to the Rapture. I go into extreme detail of the book of Revelation chapters 4 to 22 including Jesus' Rapture. This book will be a compilation from that chapter and be dedicated solely to Jesus' Rapture. There is more in this book with respect to God's earthly timeline when Jesus' second coming and the Rapture will occur with referencing from the Hebrew calendar as well as a list of events that must occur before Jesus' second coming.

Have your KJV Bible handy and let's begin.

JESUS' RAPTURE PROPHECY

Jesus prophesied in the gospel of John that he will raise all that God gave him on *the last day*; John 6:39, 40, 44, 54, 12:48. He repeats it five times. *All* means everything including every soul that God created, good and bad, since Creation. Notice in these verses from Jesus that the last three words are *the last day*. There is nothing added after "the last day". Day is in the singular not the plural. One last day not the last days.

He will raise everyone on *the last day*. There will be one final twenty four-hour day then time is no more. Time is a property of humanity and our universe. It is one fourth of our dimensionality, length, width, height and time. All of these are measurable and tangible to the universe God created for us. Humanity is finite and will end when time ends as Jesus said on *the last day* then eternity begins.

John 6:39, 40, 44, 54, 12:48 are undeniable, specific, simple and direct. They are not extrapolated conjecture, supposition and symbolism as all the Tribulation Rapture explications are.

John 6:39 Jesus says he will raise all that God gave him which includes everything as defined by Jesus in Matthew 28:18 where he declares all power is given unto him in heaven and earth. John 6:40, 44, 54 refers to those that have accepted him which will be raised on *the last day*. John 12:48 refers to those who have not accepted him who he will raise on *the last day* for judgment which is the Great White throne judgment of Revelation 20:11. Everyone good or bad will be raised on *the last day* and judged. No one is exempt from judgment. Every soul that God created from day six, Genesis 1:26-31, to *the last day* will be judged for what they did in the body; 2 Corinthians 5:10.

God determined before the creation of this universe that humanity will have a beginning and an ending. Jesus proves the ending with John 6:39, 40, 44, 54, 12:48 as well as when he wrote Revelation 21 and 22 where a new heaven, a new earth and a new Jerusalem will take its place and the sun will be no more therefore time will be no more. Genesis is the beginning of time and Revelation is the culmination of time and the transition to everlasting eternity.

And here is an interesting fact about the new heaven and new earth, if your name is in the book of life and Jesus grants you access to them then you will remember nothing of your life you had in the physical body of this world, Isaiah 65:17, nothing!

Now that we know the resurrection of humanity will be on *the last day*, the next question is when is *the last day*? Many people question these verses in John 6:39, 40, 44, 54, 12:48 and always want to add more to these verses than what Jesus said. Adding more to what Jesus said is in essence correcting the Lord. They always say the last day of what? It is not the last day of _____ fill in the blank with your own pride filled guess, it is the last day PERIOD. God has determined a finite time and Jesus will raise us all on the last day of time for judgment.

To really understand scripture is not to add or take away from it but to accept it as written by the Lord. God in Deuteronomy 4:2 and Jesus in Revelation 22:18-19 both warn NOT to add or take away from what is written or there will be serious consequences for correcting the Almighty. The word of the Lord is to be accepted verbatim, not as you want it.

Religion dogma is the essence of changing scripture to fit the pride of man. Dogma is the interpretation of scripture rather than repeating scripture. That is why there are over 38,000 Christian religions because each one believes their pride filled interpretation is more correct that the other and most of all more correct that the actual words by the author of the Bible Jesus Christ; Hebrews 12:2. Interpretations by man are full of the pride of man and God hates pride. Interpretations are why organized Christianity has failed to discern Jesus' Rapture and have injected pride to create the false Tribulation Raptures.

So, when is *the last day*, the only true Rapture? Jesus will return to this earth, His second coming, to remove the current ruler, Satan, at the end of the seven-year Tribulation and he will rule this earth you and I currently occupy for one thousand years; Revelation 20:4-6. *The last day* is at the end of Jesus' millennial reign on this earth and then time is abolished and eternity begins.

It's that simple. Clearly defined by Jesus that he will raise all on *the last day*. Jesus will return and claim this earth at his second coming at the end of the Tribulation week and rule for 1,000 years and at the end of the 1,000 years he will raise you and I out of our graves to be judged and sentenced to two places in eternity. If your name is in the book of life you enter into the new heaven. If your name is not in the book of life then you enter into the lake of fire. Both are eternal locations for souls that will be placed into a spiritual body; 1 Corinthians 15:44.

The last day is the final 24 hours of Jesus' 1,000-year reign on this earth and his millennial reign commences AFTER the 7-year Tribulation. Therefore, all Tribulation Rapture explications either pre, mid, post or anything in between, are unbiblical and if unbiblical they are blasphemy.

Jesus' Rapture prophecy is undeniable and irrefutable. One other verse in the KJV that specifically uses the three words *the last day* is John

11:24 where Martha admits to Jesus; I know that he shall rise again in the resurrection at *the last day*. John 11 is the story of Jesus raising Lazarus from the dead. By Martha's faith in Christ Lazarus was raised from the dead and she admitted that she knew all souls would be resurrected on *the last day*.

How did Martha know that the Rapture, aka resurrection, is on *the last day*? Martha was a Jew. Job knew it would be on *the last day* and I believe Job 14:12 is why Martha knew. The Jews knew the resurrection would be on *the last day* from Job. Job clearly defined it in Job 14:12 that man will sleep, or be dead, and not be raised, resurrected, until the heavens be no more. Note Job said heavens in the plural and not heaven in the singular. The heavens are that which we see with our eyes in the sky and the universe, and that which believers know exists where Jesus is with God presently.

You die and will not be raised out of your sleep, grave, until the heavens that exist now are no more, destroyed forever.

When are the heavens no more? On **the last day** of time, **the last day** of John 6:39, 40, 44, 54, 11:24, 12:48 which occurs at the end of Jesus millennial reign. Revelation 20:11 specifically says "the earth and heaven fled away; and there was found no place for them". Job 14:12 matches exactly to what Jesus scripted in Revelation 20:11, the heavens are no more and man cannot be raised until heaven and earth are destroyed.

The 7-year Tribulation is Revelation 4 to 20:4. Jesus' millennial reign is from Revelation 20:5 to 20:11. Therefore to deny Job 14:12 is to be a Tribulation Rapture adherent and calling Job the servant of God a liar. Man will not be raised until these current heavens and earth are no more.

Job 14:12 matches Jesus in John 6:39, 40, 44, 54, 12:48 exactly. The book of Job is purported to the be the oldest book in the Bible. The servant of God, Job 1:8, and the Son of God are harmonious with the last day Rapture.

Jesus affirms Job 14:12 when he says "no man hath ascended up to heaven" in John 3:13. No human that has died since creation is in heaven right now as Jesus clearly states. You don't go to heaven when you die, you sleep until Jesus raises you out of the graves on the last day. To believe you go to heaven when you die, as most Christian religions and organized churches preach today, is to deny Jesus John 3:13, John 6:39, 40, 44, 54, 12:48.

John 5:28-29 Jesus clearly states there will be one hour on one day when all in the graves will hear his voice, some to the resurrection of life and some to resurrection of damnation. Everyone good and bad! Not just the church, everyone. This is the great white throne judgment of Jesus where he judges every soul good and bad on the last day and sentences them to either the new heaven or the lake of fire which occurs at the end of Jesus' millennial reign when the heavens are no more at Revelation 20:11-15 and a new heaven and a new earth are created Revelation 21.

Jesus in John 5:28-29 affirms that there is one hour when everyone good and bad hears his voice from their graves. There is not one resurrection for the good and then another for the bad at two separate times. Jesus states one hour for everyone. There are the good and the bad in the graves right now which affirms Jesus statement in John 3:13 that no man hath ascended up to heaven.

Jesus in Matthew 25:31-46 is the sheep and goat judgment which repeats the last day Rapture and backs up what he declared in John 5:28-29. Verse 31 is Jesus declaring the great white throne judgement of Revelation 20:11 which occurs after his 1,000-year reign on earth. Verses 33-34 the sheep are placed on his right hand and the goats on the left and the sheep will inherit the Kingdom of God which doesn't occur until the new heaven, new earth and new Jerusalem are revealed in Revelation 21. Verse 41 the goats are destined for "everlasting fire" which is the lake of fire of Revelation 20:14-15, and the everlasting doesn't begin until Revelation 20:11 when this heaven and earth are gone which is after Jesus' 1,000-year reign on earth. And finally Verse 46; "And these shall go away into everlasting punishment: but the righteous into life eternal." One day on the last day when all are Raptured, judged and sentenced. There is only one judgement day for all souls, not one for the church and another one later for everyone else.

Another affirmation that souls are not in heaven, as Jesus declared in John 3:13, is Matthew 27:52-53 where saints rose out of their graves and walked around the holy city Jerusalem after Jesus' first resurrection. You and I will sleep in our graves until Jesus calls us to the Rapture judgment on *the last day* of time.

Revelation 20:4-6 is Jesus reiterating his last day Rapture for you and I mentioned in John chapters 5 and 6. Read Revelation 20:4-6 in context for the full message from Jesus. Revelation 20:5 specifically says "But the rest of the dead lived not again until the thousand years were finished. This is the first resurrection." You and I are the "rest of the dead". The first resurrection is referring to specific requirements from Jesus in Revelation 20:4 and does not include you and I but includes those killed during the Great Tribulation, the second half of the 7-year Tribulation.

There are two resurrections for humanity; the first resurrection which does NOT include you and I and the true Rapture which is you and I that occurs when Jesus' 1,000-year reign on earth is FINISHED. Jesus is undeniable in Revelation 20:5 with specificity that you and I will not be resurrected until his 1,000-year reign is finished. This verse completely shreds all Tribulation Rapture explications as I mentioned the 7-year Tribulation precedes Jesus' 1,000-year reign on earth.

Here are the four requirements for those who will be a part of the first resurrection, which occurs at the end of the 7-year Tribulation, as specified in Revelation 20:4;

1. Souls beheaded for the witness of Jesus and for the word of God.
2. Did not worship the beast.
3. Did not worship the beast's image.
4. Neither had received his mark upon their foreheads, or in their hands.

Let's go over each one of the requirements for those who are part the first resurrection which again is NOT you and I.

The first requirement; you must be beheaded for witnessing the gospel of Jesus Christ to others and also the word of God. How many of your Christian friends do you know that have been beheaded for doing this? What about all the Christians who have died of natural causes without being beheaded?

The second requirement; you must have not worshiped the beast. The beast is the Antichrist of Revelation 13:1-3. The beast only reigns for

42 months, as noted in Revelation 13:5, and his reign is the second half of the 7-year Tribulation defined by Jesus in Matthew 24:21 as the Great Tribulation. Therefore the first requirement to be beheaded are only those who were alive during the 42 month reign of the beast and they are those of faith, saints, as noted in Revelation 13:7. The church is present during the Tribulation as specified in Revelation 13:7 therefore there is NO Pre-Tribulation Rapture otherwise why would God exclude these saints during the second half of the Tribulation week?

The third requirement; did not worship the beast's image which is defined in Revelation 13:14-15. This is a statue that comes to life and to worship the image of the beast is in violation of Exodus 20:4-5 the second of the Ten Commandments.

The fourth requirement; did not receive the beast's mark on their forehead or their hands. This is the 666 mark of allegiance to the Antichrist noted in Revelation 13:16-18. 666 has nothing to do with present time. It is only administered when the beast is revealed because it is his number the number of a man; Revelation 13:18. The beast cannot be revealed until the first half requirements of the Tribulation week have been completed which includes among other things the 42 month testimony and duties of God's two witnesses; Revelation 11:3. The beast only reigns for 42 months and then wars with Jesus who at the battle of Armageddon throws him and the second beast which is the False Prophet into the lake of fire.

Jesus and another angel are the ones who perform the beheading of the remainder of saints that have not been beheaded by the Antichrist, for rejecting the 666, that are alive during the 42 months of the reign of the Antichrist; Revelation 14:12-20.

The harvest of the saints by Jesus and an angel in Revelation 14 and the beheading of the saints by the Antichrist who went to war with him, are the ONLY ones who will partake of the first resurrection. They are identified in white robes and are the ONLY souls, humans, in heaven documented in Revelation 6:11, 7:9, 13-14. They are not in heaven with the Lord right now because the Tribulation has not commenced, thus affirming John 3:13.

Notice in Revelation 7:14 the verse specifically says; These are they which came out of great tribulation. The Great Tribulation is the second half of the 7-year Tribulation and is specifically defined as the 42-month reign of the Antichrist which Jesus defined in Matthew 24:21-22 repeating Daniel 9:27 midst of the week.

Also, the first resurrected are the "elect" as noted by Jesus in Matthew 24:22. They go through the worst period of time ever in the history of humanity! The elect are NOT you and I; they are the saints that defied the Antichrist's requirements in Revelation 13 and were beheaded. The elect partake in the marriage supper of the Lamb, Revelation 19:9, NOT you and I, because you and I are not raised until Revelation 20:12!

The marriage supper of the Lamb defined is NOT a meal with all of those in the book of life resurrected with Christ to the new heaven at the last day Rapture. The marriage supper is detailed in Revelation 19:17-18 specifically as a meal consisting of all the armies of the Antichrist that Jesus and his armies from heaven have killed at the battle of Armageddon as detailed in Revelation 19:19-21. The supper is for the fowls of the air to eat those killed by Jesus and his armies.

The supper of the fowls, the marriage supper of the Lamb, is what Jesus prophesied in Matthew 24:28: For wheresoever the carcase is, there will the eagles be gathered together. Which is exactly what Jesus detailed in Revelation 19:17-21.

Jesus' bride is clearly defined in Revelation 21:9-27. Verse 9; I will show thee the bride the Lamb's wife, verse 10; the holy city Jerusalem is Jesus' bride, that in verse 24 houses the nations of them that are saved. The bride of Christ is the holy city new Jerusalem full of those who have been saved with their names written in the book of life. The marriage supper of the Lamb for the fowls of the air occurs at the end of the 7-year Tribulation at the second coming of Christ and then Jesus will rule on this earth for 1,000 years. The bride of Christ comes after time ends then eternity begins and there is no need for a marriage supper because there is no need for food in eternity!

The rest of the dead that Jesus said in Revelation 20:5 is everyone that has ever lived excluding those beheaded, killed, during the 42-month Great Tribulation reign of the Antichrist.

You and I are the rest of the dead not resurrected UNTIL Jesus finishes his 1,000-year reign on earth and as Job 14:12 prophesied the heavens are no more, which is at Revelation 20:11 the time of the Great White Throne judgment by Jesus.

> Hebrews 9:27
> And as it is appointed unto men once
> to die, but after this the judgment:

We die ONCE and after that the judgment on the last day when the heavens are no more. The verses I have shown you in this chapter are all in harmony from the Old Testament to the New Testament.

The Rapture is on the last day.

PAUL'S RAPTURE PROPHECY

Romans 1:1 **Paul**, a servant of Jesus Christ, called to be an **apostle**, separated unto the gospel of God.

In this chapter I will discuss Paul's prophecies of the Rapture which came after Jesus' Rapture prophecy in John 6, *the last day*. All of organized Christian eschatological theologians and religions have failed to discern this fact, since Jesus ascended to heaven, giving Paul's prophecy credence over Jesus' and for the most part have completely ignored Jesus in John 6:39, 40, 44, 54, 12:48. Because they ignored Jesus and put stock in Paul's epistles first, there are numerous speculative conjectures, suppositions and symbolisms as to when the Rapture will occur including the gravest error of the Pre-Tribulation Rapture. Paul did not become an apostle, as noted in Acts 9, until after Jesus finished his Passion and ascended to heaven. Paul was still persecuting Jews!

Ask yourself this question; who gave Paul his insight for his Rapture prophecy? Paul received his knowledge from the Holy Ghost; Acts 9:17. And the Holy Ghost, Jesus and God are all one in the same Spirit; 1 John 5:7. Jesus edified Paul through the Holy Ghost, therefore all of Paul's Rapture prophesies are harmonious with Jesus' Rapture prophesies as you shall soon see.

Very important; Jesus declared *the last day* Rapture in John 6:39, 40, 44, 54, 12:48 before he assigned Paul to be an Apostle to the Gentiles.

1 Thessalonians 4:13-18 is Paul's prophecy of the Rapture. Read these verses carefully in your KJV Bible. Note Paul in verse 1 of this chapter specifically addresses brethren who are the believers, the church. He is not talking to unbelievers.

Verse 13-14 Paul mentions those who sleep in Jesus, this is the dead in Christ. Again, Paul is only talking about the church. Verse 15 Paul specifically talks about those that are alive and remain unto the coming of the Lord shall not prevent, precede, them which are asleep, the dead in Christ rise first then anyone alive in Christ when he appears rise next. Verse 16 Jesus **descends** from heaven and the dead in Christ rise first. Notice Jesus has left heaven, this is important, he leaves heaven, the dead DO NOT meet him in heaven when they rise first.

Verse 17 is the critical verse; Then we which are alive and remain shall be caught up together with them **in the clouds**, to meet the Lord in the **air**: and so shall we ever be with the Lord.

Those alive at the coming of the Lord are "caught up" after the dead in Christ are "caught up". The phrase "caught up" in the Greek, the Greek is the text the KJV translators used primarily for the New Testament, is arpazo which means to be snatched up. In the Latin vulgate bible, the phrase "relinquimur simul rapiemur" translates "shall be caught up together at the same time". Rapio in Latin means to be snatched and the aforementioned phrase in the Latin vulgate bible is simplified to the English conversion to the common nomenclature that we use today to describe the resurrection of humanity; the Rapture. Arpazo in the Greek, rapio in the Latin, converted to Rapture in English, caught up!

Continuing on with verse 17; this verse specifically says that those alive will be caught up together with the dead together to meet Jesus in the clouds NOT heaven and then we will be with the Lord forever. Two important events. Jesus descends from heaven in verse 16 and then the Rapture is to the clouds in verse 17 NOT to heaven so that we can be with him forever.

Why did Jesus leave heaven to Rapture us up to the clouds? Why didn't Jesus stay in heaven and Rapture us to heaven? Because heaven is no more! You can't "ever be with the Lord" as specified in 1 Thessalonians 4:17 until there is an everlasting, a place with no time, the eternity of the new heaven and lake of fire.

Jesus left heaven and pulled us to the clouds because heaven is destroyed by fire at the last day Rapture judgment as Peter clearly defined in 2 Peter 3:7;

But the heavens and the earth, which are now, by the same word are kept in store, reserved unto fire against the day of judgment and perdition of ungodly men.

The day of judgment is Revelation 20:11 where that verse clearly says the heavens are no more and eternity cannot begin until the 1,000-year reign of

Jesus is finished and then time ends and eternity, ever be with the Lord, begins.

The true interpretation of Paul's Rapture prophecy 1 Thessalonians 4:13-18 is in complete harmony with Jesus in Revelation 20:5, 11-15. The Rapture is to the clouds not heaven, on **the last day** for the "rest of the dead" of Revelation 20:5 which is you and I, because this heaven is gone as defined in Revelation 20:11. The dead in Christ rise first and then right after them the alive in Christ rise together with them at Revelation 20:12-13 for the Great White Throne judgment.

Where the theologians and religious scholars fail with their Tribulation Rapture explications is not taking the text of 1 Thessalonians 4:13-18 verbatim and making an assumption that pulling us to the "clouds" has the same meaning as heaven when it is not. And if the Rapture is to heaven then Jesus would not have left it to pull us up to it!

1 Thessalonians 4:16-17 would have to be rewritten like this for us to be Raptured to heaven; Jesus shouts from heaven and the dead in Christ rise first: Then we which are alive and remain shall be caught up together with them in heaven, to meet the Lord in the air: and so shall we ever be with the Lord.

Understand this, this heaven and earth are going to be burned up; 2 Peter 3:10. Why would Jesus Rapture us to a heaven that will be burnt up?

This is why the KJV Holy Bible is so important because it is a transliterated translation to English, not just a translation. You have to take the Bible word for word. If you don't then you can see the pride of man working with all of their false Rapture interpretations that we are pulled up to this current heaven that Jesus occupies! Now most all of Christianity has followed the lies of the Tribulation Raptures as sheep to the slaughter.

I don't want to be Raptured to a heaven that will be burnt up! The true Rapture is not to this heaven, it is to the new heaven at Revelation 21:1.

Paul's Rapture of 1 Thessalonians 4:13-17 matches Jesus' Rapture of the last day when you accept it word for word as Jesus descends from heaven and pulls us to the clouds because this heaven is no more which occurs at Revelation 20:11 which is after Jesus' 1,000 year reign on earth when time ends on *the last day*.

Acts 17:30-33 Paul clearly states that God has appointed a day, singular, for the resurrection of the dead and continues in Acts 24:15 that there shall be a resurrection of the dead, both of the just and unjust. This is a repeat of Jesus in John 5:28-29 that I mentioned in Chapter 1. The good and the bad are resurrected at the same time. The church and the unbelievers, every soul good and bad, on the last day for judgment. Paul repeats Jesus because it was Jesus that gave him the insight.

1 Corinthians 15:50-54 Paul says we will all be changed in the twinkling of an eye, way less than a second. He is addressing the brethren, not the unbelievers as noted in verse 1 of this book, and affirms this when he says in verse 53; For this corruptible must put on incorruption, and this mortal must put on immortality. And verse 54 he says death is swallowed up in victory.

Immortality begins when time ends, this heaven is gone at Revelation 20:11 and the new heaven emerges at Revelation 21:1. Death is swallowed up in victory when death and hell deliver up the dead and both are thrown into the lake of fire as noted in Revelation 20:13-14. Revelation 20:11-15 occurs on the last day AFTER Jesus' 1,000-year reign on earth is finished as specified in Revelation 20:4-5, which affirms what Paul prophesied in 1 Corinthians 15:50-54.

Paul is repeating what Jesus taught him through the Holy Ghost. Paul and Jesus are in harmony.

DANIEL'S
PROPHECIES

Most Christians when they think of Daniel remember the story of him thrown into the lion's den. The lion's den story is the milk of the word and I will now give you the meat of the word. Half the book of Daniel is end time prophecy. Daniel is the "greatly beloved" of the Lord; Daniel 9:23, as told to him from the archangel Gabriel who is God's messenger.

In this chapter I will discuss Daniel's end time prophecies and how they are consistent to what I have already detailed in the first two chapters. God already planned everything for humanity before its foundation. The consistency of the prophecies in the Bible and the recorded history by humans proves the Bible's author and authenticity is Jesus; Hebrews 12:2.

In the book of Daniel chapter 9, he was praying his supplications to God of his people Israel and God heard his prayers and sent the angel Gabriel to inform him of future events. The archangel Gabriel is God's messenger and the archangel Michael is God's top warrior; Revelation 12:7.

What is the 70th week of Daniel? It is a seven-year period we now commonly refer to as the Tribulation week. As I have mentioned this seven-year period is broken down into two halves. The first 42 months is the time of God's two witnesses in Revelation 11:3 and the second 42 months is the Great Tribulation mentioned by Jesus in Matthew

24:21 which is the reign of the Antichrist in Revelation 13:1, 5.

Daniel 9:24-27 is the prophecy of 70 weeks of years of which 69 weeks are consecutive and the 70th week has yet to commence. The first 69 weeks have been completed which are from the going forth of the commandment to rebuild the 2nd Temple and Jerusalem, this is all detailed in the book of Ezra by the commandment of Cyrus king of Persia, until the messiah Jesus Christ was anointed as the most Holy riding into Jerusalem on a donkey. We are in the time interval between the 69th and 70th weeks.

In Daniel 9:24 Gabriel specifically says there will be 70 weeks determined upon thy people, the Jews, because he is talking to Daniel who is Jewish, and thy holy city, which is Jerusalem, to finish the following; finish the transgression, make an end of sins, reconcile iniquity, bring in everlasting righteousness, seal up the vision and prophecy, and anoint the most Holy.

None of the promises in Daniel 9:24 have come to fruition. There are plenty of transgressions continuing today. Transgressions are violations of God's laws. The transgression in the singular, as noted in verse 24, I believe is Israel's rejection of their Messiah Jesus Christ. Sin continues. Iniquity is on the increase. There is no everlasting righteousness because Satan still has power over this world as noted in Luke 4:5-8 as he clearly states in Luke 4:6 the world is "delivered unto me". Everlasting righteousness begins at the end of the Tribulation at Jesus' second coming when Jesus throws the Antichrist and the false prophet into the lake of fire and Satan into the bottomless pit for 1,000 years. Jesus is the most Holy anointed at this time and rules this earth for 1,000 years. Evil on earth is overcome and everlasting righteousness through Jesus' reign begins. The prophecy of the Rapture has not been fulfilled. The world right now is under the control of Satan.

What is the meaning of the word *week* that Gabriel refers to in Daniel 9:24? It is not a week that we commonly understand today as being a seven-day consecutive period starting with the first day of the week Sunday and ending with the seventh day of the week Saturday, which is on our common calendars today and also on the Jewish calendar. The definition of a week Gabriel is referring to is a period of seven consecutive years, a week of years. The Bible defines for us what a week of years is in Genesis 29.

Jacob meets Rachel at a well and falls in love with her. Rachel's father Laban, in Genesis 29:15, asks Jacob what his wages should be for laboring for him, as Jacob had been living and working with them a month. Jacob responds Genesis 29:18; I will serve thee seven years for Rachel thy younger daughter.

So, Jacob worked for Laban for seven years and then came to Laban to collect his wages, Laban's youngest daughter Rachel. But Laban fooled Jacob and gave him his eldest daughter Leah instead because it was the custom of the people that the firstborn should marry before the younger. Jacob finds out in the morning that the person he had in his tent during the night was not Rachel, it was Leah. Jacob approached Laban and asked him why he gave Leah instead of Rachel. Laban tells Jacob of their custom that the younger must not be wed before the elder. Laban responds to Jacob's plea to have Rachel as his second wife Genesis 29:27

> **Genesis 29:27**
> **Fulfil her week, and we will give thee this also for the service which thou shalt serve with me yet seven other years.**

Genesis 29:27 is the first mention in the Bible that a seven-year period is referencing to one week, a week of years, or as the verse is clear, fulfill her wcck is seven other years, or in seven more years Jacob will be able to claim his second wife Rachel.

This is our Bible definition as the referent of what the angel Gabriel mentions as seventy weeks in Daniel 9:24. One week, in this nomenclature, equals a period of seven consecutive years, a week of years. Therefore, to complete all the items mentioned by Gabriel in Daniel 9:24 there is a period of time of 70 weeks of which each week is a block of 7 years. To fulfill the prophecy of Daniel 9:24 a total time period of 490 years must be fulfilled, 7 times 70 weeks.

But the 70 weeks are not all consecutive, the 70th week has not commenced, as explained by Gabriel in Daniel 9:25. Gabriel says there are 69 *consecutive* weeks from the going forth of the commandment to rebuild Jerusalem, as noted in Ezra 1 by Cyrus King of Persia, and the temple and wall, until Messiah the Prince, which is a title for Jesus Christ, shall be seven weeks, and threescore and two weeks, which totals 7+60 (3x20, a score is a twenty year period) +2=69.

So Gabriel has defined in Daniel 9:25 that there are 69 consecutive weeks, or 483 years, broken down into two distinct time period sections, from the time that Jerusalem is rebuilt with the temple, both were destroyed by the Babylonians and Daniel and many Jews taken to Babylon for seventy years of captivity as noted in Daniel 9:2, until Jesus' triumphant entry into Jerusalem on the foul of an ass declaring he is the Messiah, Matthew 21:6-11 and a few days thereafter His crucifixion.

During the 69 weeks of year's period the temple is rebuilt for the second time. This is the same as the first temple Solomon constructed and destroyed by the Babylonians. It is God's house on earth, a replica of the original temple in heaven as noted in Revelation 7:15.

There are two distinct time frames of the 69 consecutive weeks that Gabriel mentioned in Daniel 9:25 and they are:

The first mention, seven weeks, is the 49-year period it took to rebuild the second temple as well as the rebuilding of the city of Jerusalem as decreed by Cyrus king of Persia. Three years the Jews were thwarted by their enemies, as detailed in Ezra 4 and 5, to begin construction of the temple and 46 years unabated construction to rebuild as noted in John 2:20.

The second mention, threescore and two weeks, is 62 weeks of years or a 434-year period from the finishing of God's temple to Jesus the Messiah riding the donkey into Jerusalem declaring He is their King and subsequent crucifixion a few days after that.

In Daniel 9:26 Gabriel clearly states the crucifixion occurs after the 62 weeks of years as he says "shall Messiah be cut off, but not for himself" which is a declaration that Jesus was forcibly killed, cut off, not for himself, as He died on the cross for humanity to take away the sin of the world. The remainder of Daniel 9:26 is the declaration that a prince shall come and destroy the city, Jerusalem, and the sanctuary, the temple, which is exactly what the Romans did in 70AD.

The Romans flattened the city and everyone in it. Jerusalem has been rebuilt over time but the temple has not. The temple will be rebuilt again for a third time as it will be standing prior to and during the 70th week.

Daniel 9:27 Gabriel says at the start of the verse, "he shall confirm the covenant with many for one week". The 'one week' at the end of this sentence is the last week of the 70 weeks prophecy by Gabriel in Daniel 9:24, it is the 70th week the Tribulation week. The 'he' in this sentence that shall confirm the covenant is Satan. Satan gives permission for the 'the covenant' to continue during the 70th week, which is God's original covenant with Israel as noted in Exodus 24:7, 34:27-28 and Hebrews 8:9.

Daniel 9:27 continues; 'and in the midst of the week he shall cause the sacrifice and the oblation to cease'. In the middle of the 70th week, half of seven is three and half years, Satan shall cause the sacrifice and the oblation to cease. Sacrifices are the religious blood rituals sacrificing to God established in Exodus 24:4-8 where Moses sacrificed an oxen and put the blood into basins and sprinkled half the blood onto an alter with twelve pillars that he had built and the other half onto the people after reading from the book of the covenant.

These rituals were originally performed in the portable tabernacle at the altar during their forty-year wilderness wanderings after being released from Egypt's bondage and also in the temple's altar in Jerusalem that Solomon built. In Exodus and Leviticus there are numerous verses explaining in detail how God wants the Jews to perform these blood sacrifices and sprinkle the blood upon the altar and other locations within the tabernacle and temple.

Oblation means to make an offer of something to God, for instance a meat offering. Oblation is first mentioned in Leviticus 2 with specificity of how a person is to perform their offering to God. The offering must be placed upon the altar by a high priest, as noted in Leviticus 2 the high priest is Moses' brother Aaron and his sons. The only way to make an oblation to God is for His house, the temple, to be standing because the offering must be performed by a Levitical priest upon the altar of God and the only place the altar of God can reside on earth is in the inner court of the temple.

This is the dilemma for the Jew today, the temple as I mentioned was destroyed in 70AD by the Romans, and has not been rebuilt. Therefore, the Jews have no ability and have not performed sacrifices and oblations as is a part of the covenant God made with His people since the destruction of the second temple. True sacrifices and oblations can only be performed in God's temple upon His altar.

In order for the prophecy of Daniel 9:27 by Gabriel, to confirm the covenant and cease sacrifice and oblations in the midst of the week, to be fulfilled, the temple must be rebuilt for a third time and standing to perform the sacrifices and oblations of Jewish customs. As of this writing the temple is not standing. It will be rebuilt, so watch and know when this starts that the time of the 70th week will be nigh at hand.

Validation that the Temple is standing during the 70th week is given again in Revelation 11:1-2 where John is told to measure it.

Paul also confirms that the 3rd Temple will be in built and in full operation prior to the 70th week in 2 Thessalonians 2:1-4 as the day of the Lord, Jesus' 2nd coming, cannot commence until there is a falling away first, which is the sacrifices and oblation ceased by Satan's command in the middle of the 70th week, and the man of sin the son of perdition, the beast of Revelation 13, aka Antichrist, is revealed in the midst of the 70th week, and the Antichrist declares he is God sitting in the Temple's Holy Of Holies, the inner court, declaring he is God.

Therefore, be a watchman and keep your eyes close on the temple mount area of Jerusalem. Currently the Muslims have built the Al-Aqsa mosque over the Dome of the Rock, the purported exact location of the original two temples. This mosque must be destroyed and the temple reconstructed at that location, as this is the exact location of the foundation of the first two temples. The Babylonians destroyed the first and the Romans destroyed the second. It is God's most sacred real estate on earth.

Ask yourself this; why would the Muslims build their mosque on the exact location of God's temple? Supposedly this is the location where Muhammad ascended to heaven. But the Muslims also knew it was the location of the second temple because the temple's foundation stones were there when they built the original Mosque in 691AD on top of those stones.

Satan's primary existence and objective is to try and thwart God's plans. The Muslims were in full knowledge that they were constructing their mosque over the original location of God's house. I will not go into great detail of why I believe Allah is Satan, suffice to say that the Quran specifically targets Jews and Christians, no other religion groups. Jews and Christians are God's own.

What greater abomination of defiance to God's authority than for Satan to construct his house directly over God's. Do you see my point? At any rate, God's temple will be rebuilt for a third time because all of Gabriel's messages of prophecy in the Holy Bible have been and will be fulfilled.

69 of the 70 weeks that Gabriel prophesied have been completed at Jesus' crucifixion and they were consecutive. The covenant for one week, the 70th week, the Tribulation, has not been confirmed by

Satan and has not commenced as we have shown from Daniel 9. We are in a time interval between the 69 and 70th weeks. The start of the 70th week will be determined by God because everything is created by Him and for his pleasure.

Daniel 11:30-45 is the 42-month reign of the Antichrist, the Great Tribulation as Jesus said in Mathew 24:21. Daniel 11:31 again confirms that the third Temple will be standing "sanctuary of strength", repeats Daniel 9:27 the daily sacrifice will be taken away, and they shall place the abomination that maketh desolate.

The abomination that maketh desolate is the Antichrist declaring he is God in the holy of holies in the third temple as Paul detailed in 2 Thessalonians 2:4 and Jesus said in Matthew 24:15-21 the Antichrist will "stand in the holy place". Jesus says to be a watchman for this event and hced his warnings! What is more abominable to God than Jesus' antithesis declaring himself as God in the third temple? NOTHING!

Daniel 11:32-35 the faithful who are not deceived by the Antichrist's flatteries, who instruct the people in righteousness and are killed by the sword, flame, by captivity and spoil many days which is the 42-month reign of the Antichrist. These are those of Revelation 20:4-5 of the first resurrection as I detailed in Chapter 1, the elect. They are "made white" in Daniel 11:35 which is direct reference to the white robes of Revelation 6:11, 7-9, 13-14.

Daniel 11:36-37 is direct reference to 2 Thessalonians 2:1-4. The abomination that maketh desolate. The Antichrist deceiving all that he is God by declaring he is God in the 3rd temple holy of holies inner court.

Daniel 11:38-45 are the events that the Antichrist performs during his 42-month reign on earth. Taking over the nations and warring with them.

Daniel 12:1 Michael the archangel, God's four star general, shall "stand up" is in direct correlation to the angel in Revelation 19:17-18, the angel who is "standing in the sun" warning of Jesus' coming on his white horse with his armies clothed in fine white linen and calling the fowls of the air to the marriage supper of the Lamb. As I mentioned in chapter 1, the marriage supper of the Lamb is not a meal with Jesus for those who meet with him in the new heaven, it is a supper for the fowls of the air who eat those earth dwellers who serve the Antichrist killed at battle by Jesus and his armies who are the elect, the first resurrected of Revelation 20:4-5.

Between Daniel 12:1 and Daniel 12:2 is Jesus' 1,000-year reign on earth as noted in Revelation 20:4-6.

Daniel 12:2 comports exactly with Jesus in John 5:28-29. Daniel specifically states; And many of them that sleep in the dust of the earth shall awake, some to everlasting life, and some to shame and everlasting contempt. This is exactly what Jesus said in John 5:28-29 and what Paul said in Acts

24:15 a resurrection of the just and unjust. Both the good and bad will be resurrected simultaneously and according to Daniel they will be resurrected to an **everlasting** life or an **everlasting** contempt. And as Jesus said in Revelation 20:4-5 the everlasting, which is eternity, doesn't happen until his thousand-year reign on this earth is finished! Daniel 12:2 everlasting is John 6:39, 40, 44, 54, 12:48 *the last day*.

Daniel 12:5-7 one on the bank asks the one clothed in linen standing on the water, I presume this to be Jesus as it is a direct reference to Jesus walking on the sea Matthew 14:25, how long shall it be to the end of these wonders, the reign of the Antichrist and his deeds, and the answer in verse 7 is time, times and half a time. A time is one year, therefore 1 year for time, 2 years for times and half year which equals 3.5 years or 42 months. Daniel 12:7 matches Revelation 13:5.

Daniel 12:10 many shall be made purified and made white and tried. These are the saints Revelation

6:11, 7:9, 13-14 of the Great Tribulation second half of the 7-year Tribulation.

Daniel 12:11 And from the time that the daily sacrifice shall be taken away, and the abomination that maketh desolate set up, there shall be a thousand two hundred and ninety days. This means from the time Satan takes away the sacrifice and oblation in the Temple, occurring during the first half of the Tribulation, until the fulfillment of the reign of the Antichrist, maketh desolate set up, is $1,290 \div 30 = 43$ months.

As you can see from what I have detailed in all the previous chapters, Job, Daniel, Jesus and Paul are all in complete harmony. Not one of them ever said the Rapture is at any time pre, mid or post Tribulation or anything in between.

JESUS' SECOND COMING AND GOD'S TIMELINE FOR HUMANITY

In this chapter I will go into further detail when Jesus's second coming will be and prophecies that remain to be fulfilled before he returns.

Hebrews 9:28; So Christ was once offered to bear the sins of many; and unto them that look for him shall he appear the second time without sin unto salvation.

I am not a date setter as no one knows the hour but God Matthew 24:36, which is a specific date and time, however I will give you the signs in detail in the next chapter as Jesus commands the faithful to be Watchmen. As I mentioned in previous chapters, Jesus' second coming is not the Rapture for you and I but only for the first resurrected at the close of the Tribulation week. Everything from Revelation 4 to 20:6 must be fulfilled and much more before Jesus returns.

I will now go over verses in the Bible that confirm God's timetable for humanity to have an understanding of when we can expect these events to occur; the Tribulation week, Jesus' second coming, Jesus' 1,000 year reign on this earth, the last day prophecy by Jesus for the true Rapture and when time will end and eternity begins.

My calendar reference will be the Hebrew calendar as it is more correct than the Gregorian Catholic calendar which has been adjusted over time to have pagan Easter fall more in line with the church's religion dogma ritual dates. The Hebrew calendar references from the first day of Creation and the Gregorian from Anno Domini, AD, or when Christ was born. The Bible doesn't record the date of Jesus' birth reference to any other calendar of that period so the exact date of Jesus' birth has no human reference point. December 25th for Jesus' birth is an arbitrary date set by the Catholic church which as there is no date defined in the Holy Bible is the contrivance of man's pride of the Roman Catholic church's continued religion objective to blend paganism with scripture as they did with Easter. See my book Testimonials of a Biblical Christian A Nonreligious Perspective of the Holy Bible chapter Good Wednesday for further explanation and documentation of the Catholic church dogma that is unscriptural.

The Hebrew calendar is more accurate than the Gregorian but none are pure because Jesus said he will come as a thief and we are to be prepared and watch for his coming; Matthew 24:42-46. And no man knows the day and hour, a specific date, as Jesus said Matthew 24:36, only God knows that date therefore this is a declaration that all calendars created by humans are not 100% correct.

Let's review 2 Peter 3:8-10. Verse 8 Peter specifically says; that one day is with the Lord as a thousand years, and a thousand years as one day. To God, who is outside the boundaries of human time, one 24-hour period is as 1,000 years. God can go back and forth in our time dimension because he created time and has control over it.

Verse 9 God is patient and wants all to come to repentance therefore there is a fixed amount time for humanity by Him for as many as possible to be saved by their own personal decision to accept Jesus. Paul in Romans 11:25 specifically says that the Jews are blinded, to the belief that Jesus is their messiah, until the fulness of the Gentiles come in. God has a specific date when the veil of blindness is lifted from Israel. I believe this occurs at Revelation 14:6-7 when an angel comes to earth and offers the final gospel of Jesus Christ to everyone which is before the pouring of the 7 vials of the wrath of God at the end of the Tribulation week. Again, these are signs, I'm not a date setter.

Verse 10 is important as the day of the Lord is ***the last day*** because the heavens and earth are burnt up as Peter details and this happens AFTER Jesus' 1,000 year reign on earth and the heavens are no more as specified in Revelation 20:11 which correlates with Jesus' last day Rapture of John 6:39, 40, 44, 54, 12:48. The second coming of Jesus is him reclaiming this earth for 1,000 years as I have mentioned is the at the end of the Tribulation week.

The importance of these verses from Peter is the declaration of one day is "as" a 1,000 years unto the Lord and that the day of the Lord, ***the last day,*** is after the heavens and earth are burnt up which is at the end of Jesus' millennium reign, this is the third coming of Christ at Revelation 20:11. The second coming is with the killed saints out of the Great Tribulation that live and reign with him a 1,000 years on this earth as priests of God and Christ; Revelation 20:6.

The second coming is at the end of the Tribulation week and he comes with the harvested saints from the Great Tribulation NOT the entire church. Jesus' bride is Revelation 21:9-10 which is the new Jerusalem and is the entire church which is not revealed until this present heaven and earth are burnt up and the new heaven with the new Jerusalem are created by God AFTER the 1,000-year reign of Christ on this earth is finished!

The third coming of Christ is the last day Rapture, the dead are raised which is you and I, and judged and then all those whose names are not in the book of life are sentenced to the lake of fire, those whose names are in the book of life to the new heaven and new Jerusalem.

From 2 Peter 3:8-10 he has established the reference that one day is as a 1,000-years unto the Lord and we know there is a fixed amount of time for humanity and time ceases in the twinkling of an eye 1 Corinthians 15:51-54 when eternity begins at Revelation 21:1. So how many 1,000 year days has God established for humanity?

The answer is from Job 7:1 the servant of God;

> **Is there not an appointed time to man upon earth? are not his days also like the days of an hireling?**

Job 7:1 specifically says there is "an appointed time to man upon the earth" and that appointed time is "like the days of an hireling". What are the days of an hireling? A hireling is someone you hire to work for you, a laborer. God established the work week for labor in the 4th commandment of the 10 commandments; Exodus 20:8-11. Verse 9; Six days shalt thou labor, and do all thy work. Labor six days and the seventh is the sabbath rest day for everyone including the hireling which God noted as the manservant and maidservant, verse 10-11. The 7th day sabbath of rest is a holy day as noted in verse 8.

Now that we know the appointed time for humanity from Job 7:1 is 7 days, six days labor and one day rest, and one day is as 1,000 years unto the Lord from 2 Peter 3:8-10, there are 7,000 years of time appointed to humanity then time ends!

The commandment for six days of labor and one day rest is repeated many times; Exodus 16:26 with the manna collection by Israel in the 40-year wilderness wanderings before the 10 commandments were established. More repetition; Exodus 23:12, Exodus 31:15-17, Exodus 34:21, Exodus 35:2, Leviticus 23:3, Deuteronomy 5:13-14, and on and on.

As I documented earlier, Jesus will return to reclaim this earth for 1,000 years with the saints harvested during the Great Tribulation period as detailed in Revelation 20:4-6 and at the end of his millennium reign is the last 24-hour day of time, the true Rapture. During this millennium reign of Christ, the Antichrist and the False Prophet have been thrown into the lake of fire; Revelation 19:20, and Satan is bound for 1,000 years; Revelation 20:1-3 in the bottomless pit, therefore the earth is at rest from evil for 1,000 years. Jesus' millennium reign is the Sabbath thousand-year day of rest fulfilling the 4th commandment!

Now that we know there will be 7,000 years of time and the sabbath millennium reign of rest is the reign of Christ for 1,000 years on this earth, we can simply conclude that the second coming of Christ will be at the start of year 6000 on the Hebrew calendar!

6,000 years man will labor, toil and trials, under the control of this world by Satan; Luke 4:5-8, and

1,000 years man will rest which is the millennial Sabbath of rest with Jesus Christ.

Notice I did not give a specific date, day and hour, but only the year of Jesus' second coming which is the year 6000. Reminder that Jesus second coming is at the end of the 7-year Tribulation. The current year of the Jewish calendar as of this writing is 5780 therefore Jesus returns in 220 years, his second coming!

We can also conclude that the 7-year Tribulation precedes Jesus coming at year 6000 which is the end of the Tribulation therefore the Tribulation week starts at year 5993.

I want to remind the reader that I am referencing the current year of human time to the Hebrew calendar which is not 100% correct but it's referent is the start at Creation and also Jesus says to be a Watchman for the signs of his return which is another statement that all human calendars are fallible. The Hebrew calendar is the most correct calendar because it is derived by the Holy Bible by a Jew and the entire Bible is Jewish from Genesis to Revelation. The Old Testament is the history of Israel and the New Testament is the history of the King of the Jews, Jesus Christ.

We are not in the end times. Nothing prophetic in the Bible is occurring today which I will go into detail in the next chapter what prophetic events must occur before Jesus' second coming.

The Epistle of Barnabas, not part of the Bible, chapter 15 goes into detailed explanation of God's timeline for humanity which mirrors the explanation I have put forth in this chapter. Barnabas was Paul's contemporary partner in the book of Acts. He was a Levite Acts 4:36 and a teacher Acts 13:1. You can find his epistle online and when you read it, as you read this book, he is definitely a teacher repeating scripture for understanding to those with an objective mind.

THE WATCHMAN'S LIST

Luke 12:37 Blessed are those servants, whom the lord when he cometh shall find watching: verily I say unto you, that he shall gird himself, and make them to sit down to meat, and will come forth and serve them.

We are not in the end times. Those who believe we are, including many Christians, blaspheme the Holy Bible. Let's review the prophesies that must be fulfilled between now and Jesus' second coming. Jesus said to be a Watchman in Matthew 24 and the signs are all given in the Holy Bible. Be a Watchman more than a date setter.

In my opinion the most important prophetic event to come will be the reconstruction of the third temple before the start of the Tribulation week. The third temple must be rebuilt as I explained in detail in the previous chapters. The coming of our Lord Jesus Christ cannot be fulfilled until the Antichrist proclaims, he is God in the third temple; 2 Thessalonians 2:1-4. All of the instruments for performing the Jewish rituals have been created and waiting for the temple to be rebuilt. For more on the current events of the progress to fulfill the rebuilding of the temple visit templeinstitute.org or templemountfaithful.org. These two websites claim the third temple will be built in our lifetime.

The second most important prophecy is Babylon will become a global economic center of power. Revelation 18 details the destruction of the "great city" Babylon and her riches are detailed in these verses; 3-all nations and the merchants are waxed rich. 7-lived deliciously. 12-gold, silver precious stones, fine linen, purple, silk, scarlet, thyine wood, ivory, precious wood, brass, iron, marble. 13-cinnamon, ointments, frankincense, wine, oil, fine flour, wheat, beasts, sheep, horses, chariots, slaves, even the souls of men are her merchandise. 15-merchants made rich by her.

Babylon was the center of all idolatry at the beginning of time. Genesis 11 the tower of Babel, Babel is Babylon, where the men built to the tower to God and then God confounded them from one language to many. The center of global trade and economic power had its origins in the area we call the Middle East today. The Babylonian Empire ruled the world at one time after the Egyptians. Then economic power shifted westward, Carthaginian, Athenian, Macedonian, Roman, through the kings of Europe and Britain, the United States, Japan post WWII and China today.

The Bible is clear in Revelation 18 that Babylon will again become the center of global economic power where it all started in the beginning. Notice how the economic power has steadily made its way westward around the globe and will return again to its place of origin! As Bible prophecy has proved itself time and again through history, Babylon will be built into a mighty city again full of riches because she must be destroyed as detailed in Revelation 18.

These are the two most important prophecies for the Watchman to look for before Jesus' second coming; the third Jewish Temple on Mt. Zion of which the Islamic Dome of the Rock must be destroyed and the third Temple built in its place and Babylon rebuilt into the center of global economic power.

Let's now examine the events from the book of Revelation chapter 5 through 20:6 that must occur before Jesus' second coming at the end of the Tribulation week:

- 5:1 – seven sealed book.
- 6:1-2 – first seal is opened. A man, bad guy, riding a white horse going forth to conquer.
- 6:3-4 – second seal is opened. A man riding a red horse that takes peace from the earth and that we should kill one another. He had a great sword.
- 6:5-6 – third seal is opened. A man on a black horse with balances that measured food, implies famine and food rationing.
- 6:7-8 – fourth seal is opened. A man on a pale horse, this horse is light green. His name is Death and Hell follows him. He kills a fourth part of the earth with a sword, hunger, death and beasts.
- 6:9-11 – fifth seal is opened. Souls of those slain for the testimony of the word of God

standing under his alter in heaven petitioning God to avenge their deaths. They are given white robes, the sign of purity. They are told to wait a little season until more of their brethren are killed "as they were", beheaded. These are souls in heaven that are slain out of the Great Tribulation 42-month reign of the Antichrist as identified in Revelation 7:13-17 wearing their white robes. Specifically killed for rejecting the commandments of the Antichrist as noted in Revelation 20:4.

- 6:12-16 – the sixth seal is opened. A great earthquake, sun was blackened and moon became *as* blood (ever seen the sun during the day become blackened by smoke from a large forest fire and the moon looks like blood from being filtered through the smoke?). Stars of heaven fell to earth. Stars are idioms for angels, in this case fallen angels. Heaven departed as a scroll when it is rolled together. Every mountain and island were moved out of their current place. Kings and every kind of man on earth fled to the caves in the mountains for protection and asked the earth to protect them from the wrath of the Lamb. These are the earth dwellers without faith.

- 7:1 – All winds on the earth are stopped by four angels.
- 7:2-8 – An angel seals the servants of God in their foreheads. 144,000 Jews, 12,000 each from the tribes of Israel; Juda, Reuben, Gad, Asar, Nephthalim, Manasses, Simeon, Levi, Issachar, Zabulon, Joseph, Benjamin.
- 7:9-10 – A great multitude of souls from every nation, kindreds, peoples and tongues (languages) stood before the Lamb and the throne in heaven clothed in white robes. These are souls in heaven that are slain out of the Great Tribulation 42-month reign of the Antichrist as clearly identified in Revelation 7:13-17 wearing their white robes. Specifically killed for those acts noted in Revelation 20:4. The same souls identified in Revelation 6:9-11.

- 8:1 – seventh seal is opened and heaven is silenced for about half an hour.
- 8:2 – seven angels given 7 trumpet judgments.
- 8:7 – first trumpet sounds. Hail and fire mixed with blood fall to the earth, one third part of all trees burnt up and all green grass burnt up.
- 8:8-9 – second trumpet sounds. A great mountain burning with fire is cast into the sea. One third of the sea became blood, one third of all sea life died and one third of all ships in the sea were destroyed.
- 8:10-11 – third trumpet sounds. A burning star named Wormwood falls to earth upon one third part of the rivers and the fountains of waters (aquifers) and makes the water bitter and kills many men.
- 8:12 – fourth trumpet sounds. A third part of the sun, moon and stars are darkened so that a third part of the day and night did not shine.

- 8:13 – the next three trumpets are woes; grievous distress, affliction, or trouble.

- 9:1-12 – the fifth trumpet sounds. An angel falls from heaven and has a key to the bottomless pit. He opens it and smoke rises out and darkens the sun and air. Locusts come out and they are commanded not to hurt anything green but to only hurt those men who have not the seal of God in their foreheads, which is everyone except the 144,000 Jews who were sealed in Revelation 7:2-8. They are to hurt them 5 months as with the pain of a scorpion sting. The men tormented shall seek death but they shall not find it. The locusts' have a king named Apollyon.

- 9:13-21 – the sixth trumpet sounds. Four angels are loosed out of the river Euphrates and are prepared to kill a third part of men for thirteen months, a day and an hour. Along with the angels is an army of 200 million horsemen with horses that breathed fire and brimstone. These three, the four angels, 200 million horsemen and their horses, killed a third part of men on earth with fire, brimstone and smoke which issued out of their mouths. The other two thirds of the men that were not killed on earth repented not that they should not worship devils, idols of gold, silver, brass, stone, wood and neither repented of their murders, sorceries, fornications and thefts.

- 10:1-7 Seven Thunders utter their voices but John is told not record what they said. When the 7th angel of the seven Thunders utters his voice the mystery of God shall be finished and time ends. Time ends when Jesus' 1,000-year reign on earth is finished. Therefore the 7th thunder is reserved for the last day, then time is no more. We don't know when Thunders one to six will utter, therefore they may or may not utter their messages before Jesus return. I included them here as reference to listen when they do appear.

- 11:1-14 is the finishing of the sixth trumpet. John is assigned to measure the temple of God and the alter, this is the Third Temple as I mentioned earlier in this chapter. It will be standing and the Jews will perform their sacrifices and oblations in it. The outside court is given unto the Gentiles to tread under foot 42 months. God assigns two witnesses, most believe these two are Moses and Elijah, to prophesy for him for the first half of the Tribulation, 42 months, 1260 days. If any man hurt them, they can kill by breathing fire from their mouths. They can stop rain, turn water to blood and create plagues. When their testimony is finished, the first half of the 7-year Tribulation, the beast that rises out of the bottomless pit, Apollyon, will kill them. They lay dead in the street in the great city which is where Jesus was crucified, Jerusalem, for 3 days then are brought back to life by God. They ascend up to heaven in a cloud and a great earthquake where a tenth part of the city was destroyed and 7,000 men killed.

- 11:15 the seventh trumpet sounds harking in the Third Woe which includes the pouring out of the 7 vials of the wrath of God and the 42-month reign of the Antichrist. But at the start of the trumpet sounding is a declaration that the kingdoms of the world become the kingdoms of God and of his Christ.

From Revelation 11:15 to 19:20 is the detail of the Third Woe, the second half of the Tribulation week, the 42-month reign of the Antichrist.

- 11:18 – The nations are angry because their wrath has come, the 7 vials of plagues. The time of dead will be judged, this is the dead killed during the Tribulation and judged at Revelation 20:4 not the final judgement for you and I at *the last day* Rapture judgment Revelation 20:11-15. Reward is given unto those killed during the Tribulation the prophets, saints and the faithful, and their reward is coming back with Jesus in Revelation 19 to destroy those on earth who followed the Antichrist and to become kings and priest with Jesus for 1,000 years on this earth as noted in Revelation 20:6, they are the first resurrected.

- 11:19 - And the temple of God was opened in heaven, and there was seen in his temple the ark of his testament: and there were lightnings, and voices, and thunderings, and an earthquake, and great hail.

- 12:1-2 - The woman is Israel; the sun and the moon are referenced to Jacob and Rachel and the twelve stars are the twelve tribes of Israel. The referent to these symbols is the dream Joseph had in Genesis 37:5-11. The child in Revelation 12:2 is Jesus.

- 12:3-6 – The great red dragon is Satan. Satan casts a third of the stars, these are fallen angels, to the earth. The dragon was ready to devour the child ready to be born of the woman, Israel, a man child who is Jesus who was caught up to God and his throne. Then Israel is taken unto the wilderness to a place prepared by God for 1,260 days, or the 42-month reign of the Antichrist the Great Tribulation, and she is sheltered from the wrath of the Antichrist and all that he performs during his reign.

- 12:7-17 – Satan, the dragon, is cast out of heaven to the earth forever. Satan has access to heaven and earth right now and runs the governments of the world today as he offered them to Jesus Luke 4:5-8. As of Revelation 12:9 Satan and his angels are cast out of heaven and cannot return after warring with archangel Gabriel in heaven. Gabriel is always a warrior for God. Notice who is still calling the shots for everything, God. God controls everything. This casting out of heaven is at the mid-week of the Tribulation. Satan goes after the woman which is Israel but she is protected from a flood by Satan by the earth and then goes into the wilderness for a time, times and half a time. A time is 1 year, therefore time, times and half a time are 1+2+0.5= 3.5 years. This is a repeat from the above verses of the Great Tribulation last half 42-month reign of the Antichrist. Israel during the reign of the Antichrist is protected from the events during this period. Satan then makes war with the remnant of Israel who keep the commandments of God and the testimony of Jesus Christ.

- 13:1-4 – The beast aka Antichrist is revealed at mid-week rising out of the sea. The earth dwellers worship Satan who gives the beast his power.

- 13:5-6 – The Antichrist blasphemes God, his tabernacle and those in heaven. Verse 5 also declares the term of his reign, 42 months. The Antichrist MUST reign on this earth during this Great Tribulation period as defined by Jesus in Matthew 24:21 for 42 months before Jesus' second coming because Jesus wars with him at the end of his term.

Notice in verse 6 the beast blasphemes God's tabernacle, this is another reference that the 3rd Temple will be built and in operation before he is revealed, confirming Paul in 2 Thessalonians 2:4.

- 13:7-10 – The Antichrist is warring with the saints during the second half Great Tribulation! If as the Pre-Tribulation people believe the church is Raptured to heaven before the Tribulation week then why would God leave these saints behind? These are saints, not your average person of faith. The Antichrist then is given power over all kindreds, tongues (languages) and nations. Notice in the scripture it says *given him* to kill the saints and *given him* power over the people. The Antichrist didn't earn it, he was given these powers from the dragon who is Satan and Satan cannot do anything unless God allows it. Reference Job chapter 1, Satan could not do anything to Job the servant of the Lord except when God allowed it. God calls all the shots because he created all.

- 13:11-18 – These verses represent the second beast that comes out of the earth which is the False Prophet. He has all the power of the Antichrist and causes the earth dwellers to worship the Antichrist. He has great powers and deception. He causes the earth dwellers to create an image of the Antichrist and he brings the image to life and makes it speak and also kills anyone that doesn't worship the image of the Antichrist. The False Prophet causes everyone to receive a mark on their right hand or foreheads and they cannot buy or sell unless they have the mark, name or number of the Antichrist. The number of the Antichrist is the number of a man and his number is 666. The False Prophet installs and instigates the number of the Antichrist which is 666. At no other time in history is this mark valid until the False Prophet is revealed. 666 is a mark of allegiance to the Antichrist. The Antichrist and false prophet are only on earth for 42 months commencing at the middle of the Tribulation week. 666 has nothing to do with ANYTHING at any time in history but during the reign of the Antichrist and False Prophet. Anyone that correlates anything to the 666 mark in present time blasphemes scripture. And if you blaspheme any portion of the book of Revelation you are subjected to the punishment by Jesus in Revelation 22:18-19. I suggest you read those verses very carefully and adjust your prejudices accordingly or suffer the consequences if you believe in anything that is not verbatim in the book of Revelation.

- 14:1-5 – Jesus standing on Mt. Zion with the 144,000 Jews. They follow him where ever he goes.
- 14:6-7 – An angel makes the final offer of the gospel of Jesus Christ to everyone on earth. This is what Jesus prophesied in Matthew

24:14. The last offer of the gospel before the wrath of God is poured out. The hour of judgment has come.

- 14:8 – Another angel announces the fall of the Babylon directly after the previous angel that offered the gospel. These two announcements are contemporaneous. Babylon is destroyed as I mentioned earlier which is Revelation 18.

- 14:9-11 – The third angel after the previous two announced that if anyone worships the image of the Antichrist or takes his 666 mark on their right hand or forehead, the wrath of God will be poured upon them and their final destiny is the lake of fire in eternity.

- 14:12-20 – Jesus and another angel kill all the remaining saints on the entire earth who kept the commandments of God and the faith of Jesus. This is the harvest of the saints. These are those soles in heaven mentioned in Revelation 6:11 as the fellow servants that should be killed as they were, beheaded. These are the same mentioned in Revelation 7:9, 13-14. The only souls in heaven in the entire Bible are these souls killed, beheaded during the Tribulation. Exactly what Jesus said in John 3:13; no man hath ascended up to heaven. The only time souls enter heaven is during the Tribulation and they must be killed or beheaded, not died of natural causes. This is Jesus' army he will bring with him in Revelation 19 to the marriage supper of the Lamb.

- 15:1-8 - Seven angels came out of the temple, having the seven plagues, clothed in pure and white linen. This is the announcement of the seven angels being given the 7 vials of the wrath of God. At this announcement the Third Temple will be filled with smoke from the glory of God and his power and no man can enter the temple until the 7 plagues of the 7 angels are fulfilled. Be a Watchman. The 3rd Temple filled with smoke harkens the 7 vials of the wrath of God!

- 16:1-21 – The seven angels are commanded to perform their duty and pour out the 7 vials of the wrath of God upon the earth where only those who rejected the gospel of Christ and serve the Antichrist remain! The first vial; noisome and grievous sore upon the men with the 666 mark and who worshiped the image of the Antichrist. The second vile; poured into the sea and it became as the blood of a dead man and every living soul died in the sea. The third vile; poured out his vial upon the rivers and fountains of waters; and they became blood. The fountains of waters are aquifers. The fourth vile; an angel pours his vile on the sun and power was given unto him to scorch men with fire. The scorched men repented not and blasphemed God. The fifth vile; poured out his vile upon the seat of the Antichrist and his kingdom was full of darkness. They blasphemed God for their pain and sores and repented not of their deeds. The sixth vial; poured onto the river Euphrates and the river was dried up to prepare the way for the kings of the East. Three unclean spirits come out of the mouths of Satan, the Antichrist and the False prophet which are spirits working miracles who go forth and gather the kings of the whole earth to a place called Armageddon to prepare for the battle of that great day of God Almighty. The seventh seal; poured his vial into the air and a great voice came out of the temple of heaven saying "It is done!". Then came voices, thunders, lightnings and a great earthquake greater than any earthquake since the creation. Babylon is divided into three parts and the cities of the nations were crushed. Every island fled away and the mountains were not found. Hail fell on the earth each about the weight of a talent (about 75lbs) and the men still blasphemed God.

- 17:1-18 – The judgment of the great whore, the city of Babylon. Her identity is detailed in this chapter. Ten kings are given power for one hour from the Antichrist to make war with the Lamb, aka Jesus.

- Revelation 18; As I detailed earlier, at the start of this chapter, is the second most important event for a Watchman. Babylon will be an economic global power in which all the kings of the earth perform commerce with her.

- Revelation 19; the marriage supper of the Lamb and the battle of Armageddon. I discussed this in detail in chapter 1. ***This is the second coming of Christ.*** As a reminder from the previous chapter the Antichrist and the False Prophet are defeated by Jesus and his armies, which are the killed saints from the Tribulation period, and they are thrown alive into the lake of fire where they will be forever.

- 20:1-6 – I detailed these verses in chapter 1. The identity of the souls in heaven are those who are out of the Great Tribulation who were killed and beheaded for the witness of

Jesus and the word of God, not worshipped the Antichrist nor his image and not taken the 666 mark. They lived and reigned with Jesus on this earth for 1,000 years as priests. They are the first resurrected. You and I are the **rest of the dead** verse 5 not Raptured until the 1,000-year reign of Christ on earth is finished, **the last day** of John 6:39, 40, 44, 54, 12:48.

This concludes the prophetic events that must happen in Revelation 5 to 20:6, the Tribulation period, before Jesus returns for a second time to battle at Armageddon with the Antichrist's armies.

To believe we are in the end times is to deny all of these events and Jesus is clear, to add or remove anything from the book of Revelation is to correct him and the punishment for doing so is detailed in Revelation 22:18-19. Read those verses very carefully and heed them.

EPILOGUE

I have given you nothing more than what Jesus already declared in John 6 that he will raise us all, good and bad, on the last day of time for judgment and then sentence all to our everlasting locales in either the new heaven for those in the book of life or the lake of fire for those who rejected the gospel.

Nothing in this book is conjecture, supposition, extrapolation, symbolism or best guess. The evidence in this book is irrefutable because I have repeated Jesus, Paul, Daniel, Job, John, Matthew, Luke and Peter who are all in harmony. I have connected the verses from each of them for you to have the true understanding of the resurrection of humanity which is Jesus' *the last day* Rapture.

I wrote this book because all of organized Christianity is being taught false scripture of a pre, mid or post Tribulation Rapture. I was compelled to set the record straight and to serve the Lord with accuracy and truth. If you reject the information in this book then you fail the Lord because I have repeated him.

If you accept the evidence I have presented in this book as the truth and if your church or religion has failed to discern the second most important event in human history to come, Jesus' last day Rapture, and they continue to preach a pre, mid or post Tribulation Rapture, then ask yourself what other false things are they preaching to you and why are you still following false teachers?

Believe what you may but in all things validate what you hear with the Holy Bible, refer to Acts 17:11. God will hold you accountable for what his Bible says at the judgment, not what your religion, church, Pastor, Priest, Pope, Bishop, Cardinal, Friar, Deacon or myself preaches. The Holy Bible is your absolute final authority because it was written by God.

If you seek a deeper study of the Holy Bible get my book Testimonials of a Biblical Christian A Nonreligious Perspective of the Holy Bible. Available in all formats at hundreds of bookstores and online worldwide.

APPENDIX A

Current Jewish Year: 5780
Current Gentile Year: 2020

Job 7:1 Is there not an appointed time to man upon earth? are not his days also like the days of an hireling?

2 Peter 3:8 But, beloved, be not ignorant of this one thing, that one day is with the Lord as a thousand years, and a thousand years as one day.

Jesus 2nd Coming/Battle of Armageddon.
AntiChrist and False Prophet put in lake of fire.
Satan thrown into bottomless pit.
First Resurrection.

Satan loosed from prison then thrown into lake of fire.
Heaven & Earth burnt up.
Judgment on "the last day" of LINEAR TIME in the clouds

RAPTURE
ALL SOULS

NEW HEAVEN
NEW EARTH
NEW JERUSALEM

ETERNITY

1000 YEAR REIGN OF JESUS ON EARTH
Saints harvested by Jesus and an angel in Revelation 14, during the Great Tribulation, return and reign with Jesus: Revelation 20:4

YEAR 7000 JEWISH CALENDAR
Linear Time Ends

YEAR 6000 JEWISH CALENDAR
Since Creation. Final Jubilee Year

MIDDLE OF THE WEEK
Two Witnesses   Satan cast out of
Raptured to   heaven to earth
Heaven   forever

THIRD WOE
Reign of AntiChrist
& False Prophet
Era of 666
7 Vials Wrath of God

GREAT TRIBULATION
3.5 Years

God's Two Witnesses
7 Seals 7 Trumpets

3.5 Years

TRIBULATION WEEK
70th Week of Daniel 9:27
Week of years, 7 year period.

-THIRD TEMPLE STANDING
-BABYLON WORLDWIDE
FINANCIAL POWER.

LINEAR TIME

91

Printed in the United States
By Bookmasters